Experiments with
ELECTRICITY AND
MAGNETISM

TREVOR COOK

PowerKiDS
press™

New York

Published in 2009 by The Rosen Publishing Group, Inc.
29 East 21st Street, New York, NY 10010

Editor: Alex Woolf
Designers: Sally Henry and Trevor Cook
Consultant: Keith Clayson
U.S. Editor: Kara Murray

Picture Credits: Sally Henry and Trevor Cook

Every attempt has been made to clear copyright. Should there be any
inadvertent omission, please apply to the publisher for rectification.

Library of Congress Cataloging-in-Publication Data

Cook, Trevor, 1948–
  Experiments with electricity and magnetism / Trevor Cook.
     p. cm. — (Science lab)
  Includes index.
  ISBN 978-1-4358-2807-0 (library binding) — ISBN 978-1-4358-3220-6 (pbk.)
ISBN 978-1-4042-8025-0 (6-pack)
  1. Electricity—Experiments—Juvenile literature. 2. Magnetism—
Experiments—Juvenile literature. I. Title.
  QC527.2.C65 2009
  537.078—dc22
                              2008032716

Printed in the United States

Contents

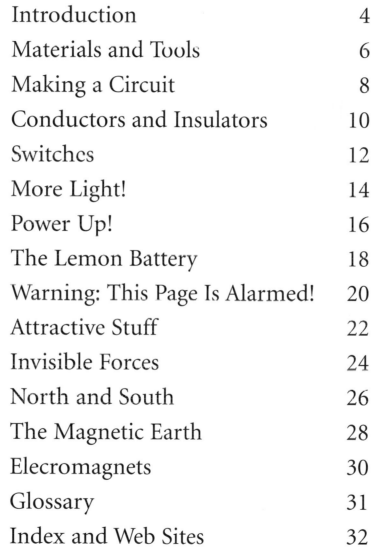

Introduction

From the earliest times, people have seen and heard the power of electricity.

Now electricity is necessary for modern life. Look around your home. Count how many things you can find that work by electricity.

How many of these things need electricity to work?
How many of these things have *magnets* in them?

brains

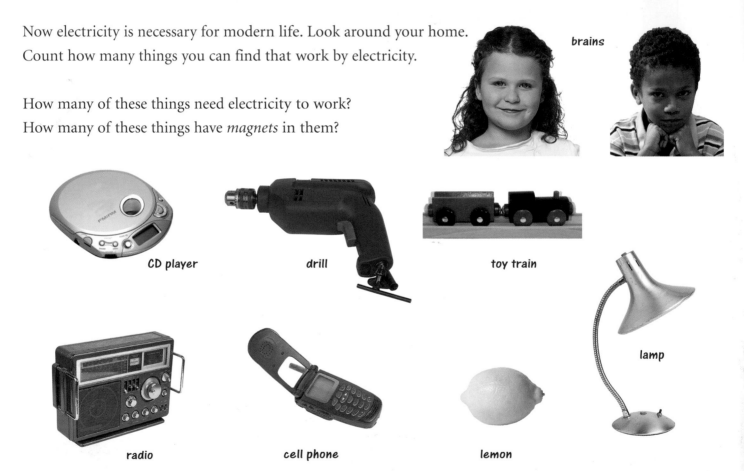

CD player

drill

toy train

lamp

radio

cell phone

lemon

Answers: They all need electricity to work except the lemon. We'll be using the lemon to make electricity later on in the book.

Anything that has an electric motor or a loudspeaker has magnets. So there are no magnets in the lamp (or the lemon!). The toy train has magnetic couplings – we'll need them on page 27.

We make electricity from other forms of energy. We can burn fuel, such as coal or oil, or use natural forces such as wind or water.

Electricity is carried to where it is needed by metal cables. The cables are held up on big towers called pylons. The thicker the cables, the more electricity they can carry.

In our home, we connect things to this supply of electricity through plugs and *sockets*, and the electricity flows through smaller wires.

In our experiments we're going to use *batteries*. Later on, we'll make our own electricity (see page 18).

Long ago, *magnetism* was thought to be a form of magic. Early navigators, such as the Vikings, used special pieces of magnetic rock, called lodestone, as simple *compasses* to help them find their way in strange seas.

Looking at magnets starts on page 22. You will need a compass when you get to page 26.

a piece of lodestone

Some technical or unusual words, shown in *italic* type, are explained in the glossary on page 31.

Materials and Tools

You should easily find many things that you need for our experiments around the house.

20 minutes This tells you about how long a project should take.

This symbol means you might need adult help.

Wire The kind of wire found inside power cords of domestic appliances is generally ideal. Ask an adult if there is one you can take apart. Ask an adult to take off the outer covering for you. Inside you'll find two or three colored wires. If you need stiffer wire, as in the coil experiment on page 30, use lighting wire. Ask an electrician for extras!

Bulb holder You need one of these for each bulb you use. Buy them at the same time as your bulbs.

Circuit board This can be made of anything that you can easily stick components to.

Batteries We've used a size that's called AA. It's a very common size and you'll find them used in lots of things around the home.

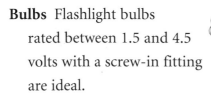

Glue stick is mostly used for sticking paper to paper.

Rubber cement is a rubbery glue that sticks most things to most other things!

Tape We use tape to hold things in position. Masking tape or clear packing tape will do.

Bulbs Flashlight bulbs rated between 1.5 and 4.5 volts with a screw-in fitting are ideal.

Buzzer Find one that works on low voltages – around 2–3 volts.

Magnets Most of our magnetism experiments use *bar magnets*, but horseshoe magnets work just as well.

Iron filings These are usually sold in a clear plastic container. You can see the effects of magnetism without opening it.

Compass A small toy compass is great for these experiments.

Lodestone You can find pieces in museum shops or on the Internet.

Copper tubing is an excellent source of copper. Get an adult to ask a friendly plumber for extras – they're often thrown away!

Friends can help
Do the experiments with your friends!

Digital LCD clock or calculator They are sold in supermarkets or drugstores and are often quite cheap! The great thing is that they don't need much electricity to make them work. You can get them to work on tiny currents.

Wire stripper In the experiments you'll always need to have the metal *conductor* exposed at the end of the wires. This hand tool is used to remove insulation. You might have one in your household tool kit. Get an adult to help you do this!

Scissors Use safety scissors that you can keep for all your experiments. Keep them away from young children.

Hammer Most homes have a hammer somewhere. Be careful when you use it and put it away when you've finished!

Making a Circuit

20 minutes

Electricity is carried in a *circuit*. The power lines on page 5 and the power cords on page 6 are all parts of circuits.

The plan

We are going to make our own circuit.

You will need:

- insulated wire
- bulb and bulb holder
- tape
- battery
- board
- scissors
- paper clips
- drawing pins

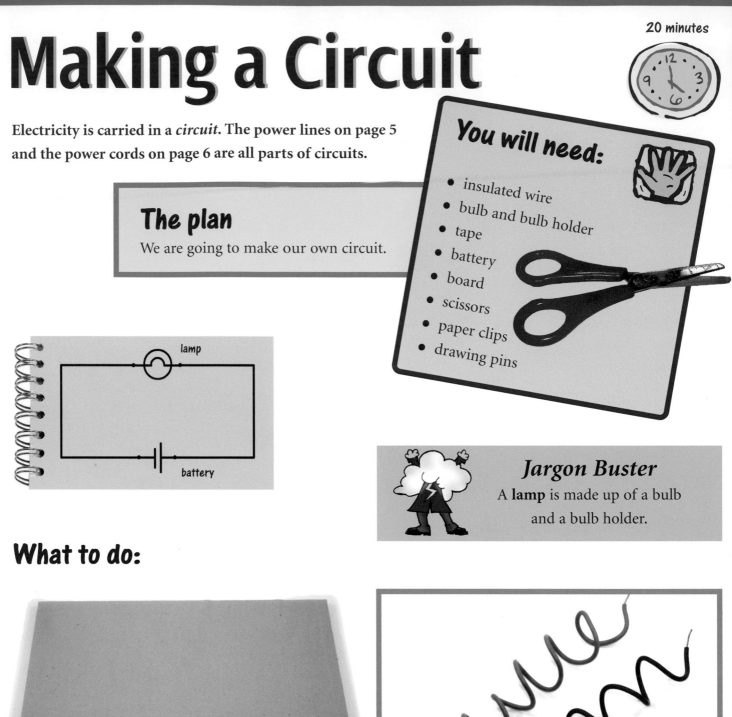

lamp

battery

Jargon Buster

A **lamp** is made up of a bulb and a bulb holder.

What to do:

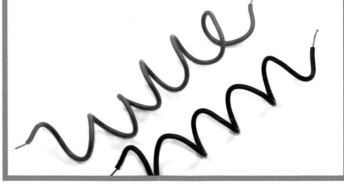

1 We need a board to build our circuit on. This is a thick piece of cardboard. You could use wood or plywood. Make it about 12 x 8 inches (300 x 200 mm).

2 Prepare your wire by stripping the colored insulation from both ends.

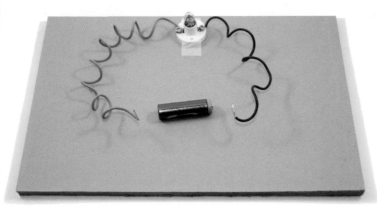

3 We've fixed the lamp to the board with some tape to make things tidier.

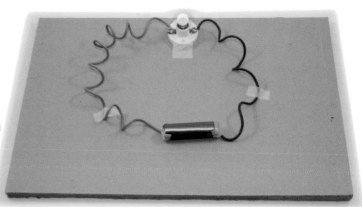

4 Fix one end of each wire to the lamp and the other ends to the battery using tape.

What's going on?

The lamp comes on because we've made a continuous circuit connecting the battery and lamp.

What else can you do?

Use two paper clips (not plastic coated) and two thumbtacks to make a battery holder like this.

The battery should be held firmly in place between the paper clips.

You can also use a battery holder to give a dependable fixing point for the wires.

Jargon Buster
Completing the circuit means allowing the current to flow.

Conductors and Insulators

Which materials can electricity pass through? Those which allow electricity to pass through are called conductors. Those that don't are called *insulators*.

35 minutes

The plan

We take the circuit we built on pages 8 and 9 and use it to find out whether materials are conductors or insulators.

You will need:

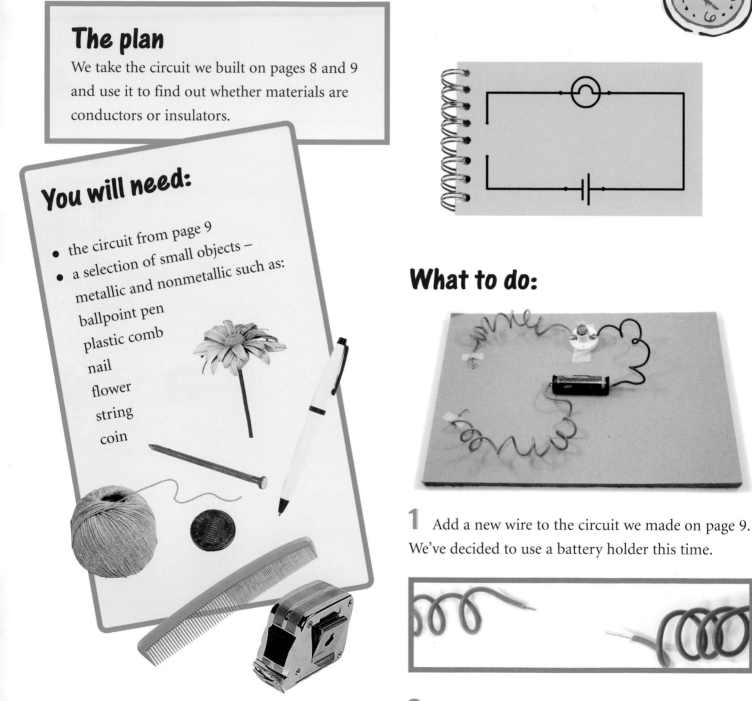

- the circuit from page 9
- a selection of small objects — metallic and nonmetallic such as:

  ballpoint pen

  plastic comb

  nail

  flower

  string

  coin

What to do:

1 Add a new wire to the circuit we made on page 9. We've decided to use a battery holder this time.

2 We are going to use the ends of the wire to test different materials.

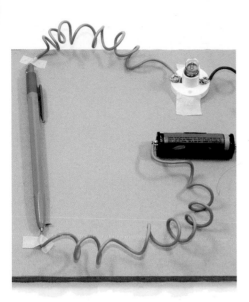

3 A plastic pen doesn't complete the circuit.

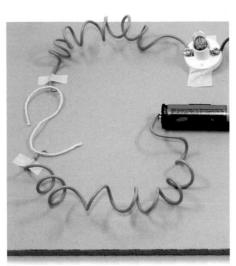

4 Neither does the string.

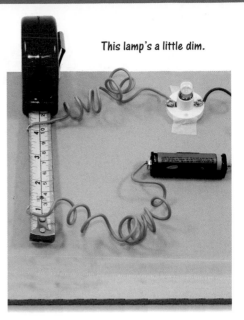

This lamp's a little dim.

5 The paint on the tape measure is resisting the current.

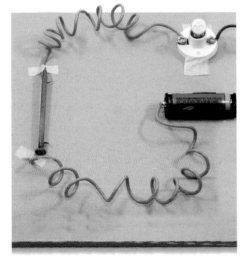

6 This nail is made of iron.

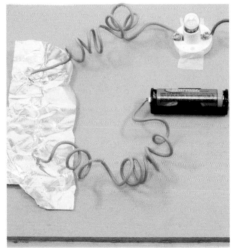

7 Here's a piece of tin foil.

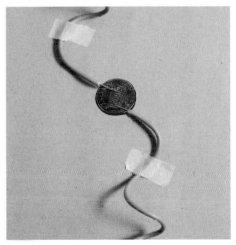

8 Will this coin complete the circuit? What about the flower?

What's going on?

Most conductors are metal. We use insulators, such as plastics, to stop electricity going where we don't want it to go.

What else can you do?

Look at these tools. Why do you think they've got thick rubber or plastic handles?

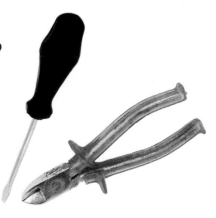

Switches

We've made a circuit that lights lamps but we probably don't want it to be on all the time.

The plan

Let's make a simple switch to turn the lamp on and off.

You will need:

- the circuit we made in the previous pages
- 2 thumbtacks
- a paper clip

30 minutes

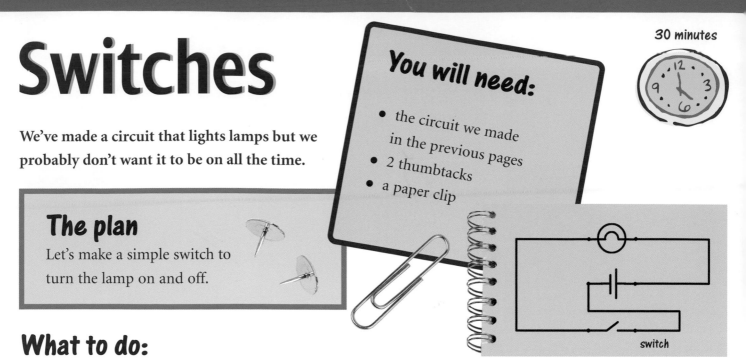

switch

What to do:

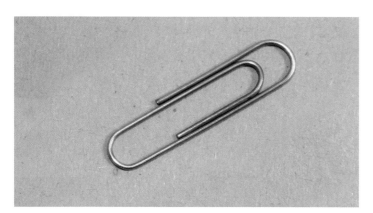

1 Your paper clip must be made of metal and not painted or coated with plastic.

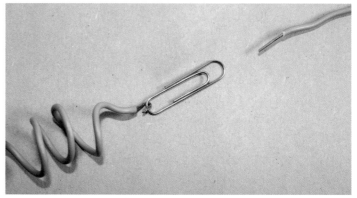

2 Test the paper clip as a conductor by the method we used in the last experiment.

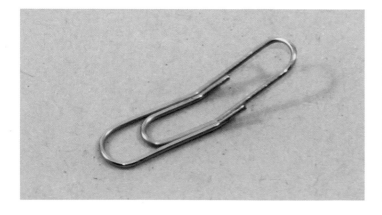

3 Bend the paper clip a little in the middle.

4 Bend the bare wire end of one of the wires around a thumbtack and press it into the cardboard.

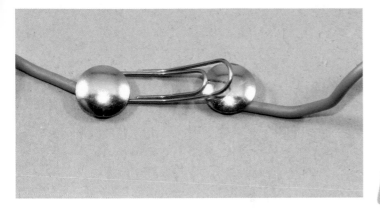

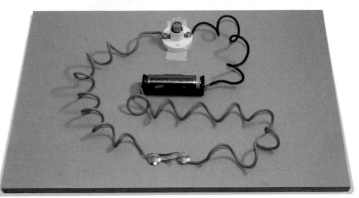

5 The other thumbtack holds the other wire and the paper clip in place.

6 Here's the switch in the circuit.

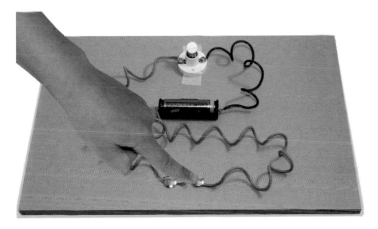

7 Press the switch to turn the lamp on!

What's going on?

Current flows when there's no break in the circuit.

Jargon Buster
Closing the switch means completing the circuit and allowing the current to flow.

What else can you do?

We made a switch that has to be held down to keep the switch closed. You can use the same components to make a switch that stays closed.

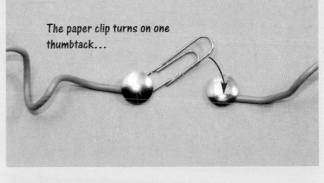

The paper clip turns on one thumbtack...

...until it rests on the other thumbtack to close the circuit.

More Light!

40 minutes

What happens when we want more light? Do we make more circuits like the one on the last page, or can we just add more lamps to the circuit? Let's find out!

You will need:

- the circuit from the last experiment
- 2 more bulbs and lamp holders
- 2 short lengths of wire with insulation stripped from the ends

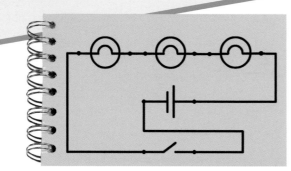

The plan

We are going to connect more bulbs to the circuit.

Experiment 1

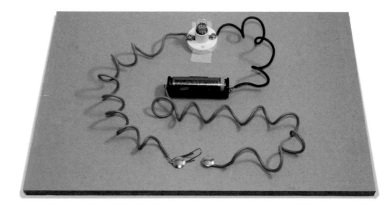

1 Take the circuit we made last time. Make sure the switch is turned off.

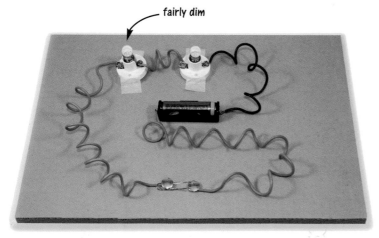

fairly dim

2 Connect another lamp in the circuit next to the first one. Switch on the current.

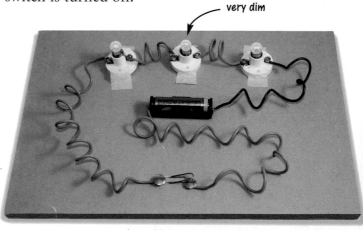

very dim

3 Switch it off and connect another lamp to the circuit to make three. Switch it on again.

What's going on?

We've connected the bulbs together in the circuit. This is called *in series*. Every bulb we add to the circuit increases the energy required for the electricity to flow.

Lamps in series

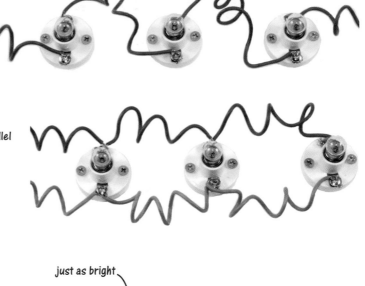

Experiment 2

There's another way to use electricity in a circuit, *in parallel*. Let's see what difference it makes to the result.

Lamps in parallel

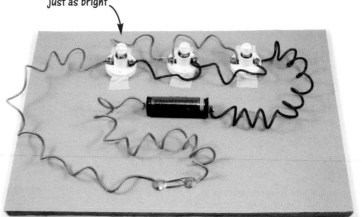

very bright

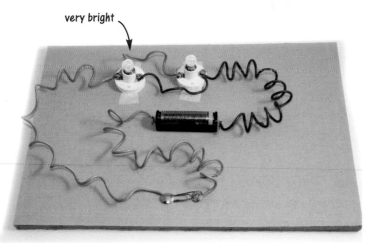

just as bright

1 Start as in step 1 on page 14. Connect one more lamp, using two more wires. Switch it on.

2 Switch it off and connect a third lamp with two more wires. Switch it on again.

What's going on?

This time we've connected the lamps in parallel. Each bulb in the circuit gets the right amount of electricity to make it work. The battery might not last for long running three bulbs, though.

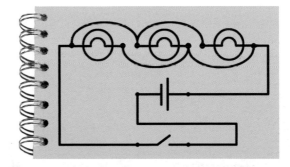

What else can you do?

We wanted more light, so it seems we'll need more power! Let's look at batteries in the next section.

Jargon Buster
A **terminal** is the means of connecting wires to devices like batteries and lamps.

Power Up!

How do we add more power to the circuit? Is there a clue in looking at the different ways the lamps worked in the circuit?

35 minutes

You will need:

- the circuit from the last experiment
- 2 thumbtacks, a paper clip
- 4 wires

The plan

Let's try connecting more batteries to the circuit in different ways.

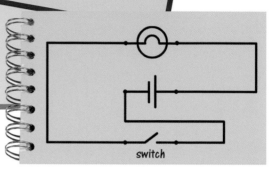

switch

What to do:

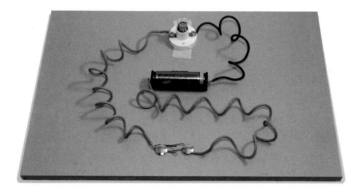

1 Start with the circuit as in step 6 on page 13.

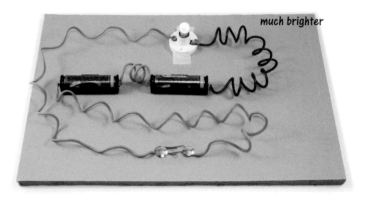

much brighter

2 Connect a second battery into the circuit. Switch it on.

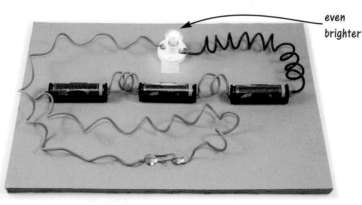

even brighter

3 Add a third battery to the circuit. The lamp is much too bright now. It might burn out!

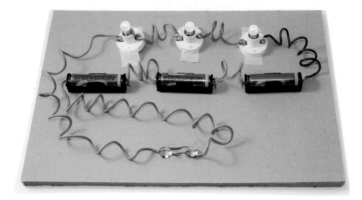

4 Try adding more lamps in series.

very dim again

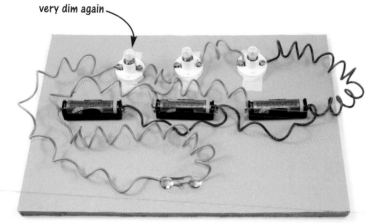

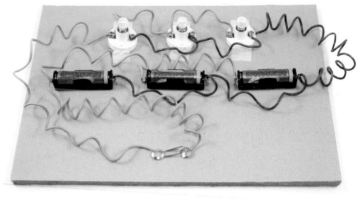

5 Now connect the batteries in parallel, as you did with your lamps on page 15.

6 Now connect together both the lamps and the batteries in parallel.

What's going on?

Adding more batteries makes one lamp burn brighter, but it will soon burn out. Connecting batteries and more lamps in parallel produces more light without it burning out.

What else can you do?

Wire components together partly in series, partly in parallel. Try combinations and predict the result.

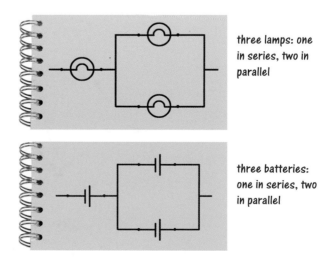

three lamps: one in series, two in parallel

three batteries: one in series, two in parallel

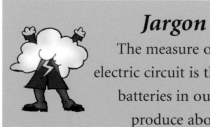

Jargon Buster
The measure of energy in an electric circuit is the **volt**. The small batteries in our experiments produce about 1.5 volts.

The Lemon Battery

40 minutes

When you've become tired of buying fresh batteries for your experiments, here's a way of making your own. The trouble is, you may have to buy some lemons instead!

The plan

We are going to produce electricity and power a device using fresh fruit!

You will need:

- three popsicle sticks
- aluminum foil
- 3 lemons
- 8 paper clips
- 3 pieces of copper tube about 4 inches (100 mm) long
- insulated wire
- device such as an old clock or calculator with an LCD display
- small knife

What to do:

1 Get an adult to cut a square hole and a slot in each lemon with a small knife.

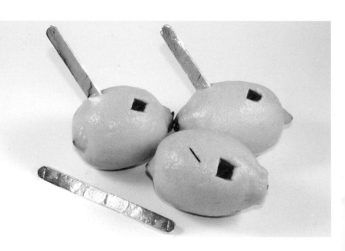

Jargon Buster

Close the circuit means the same as **switch it on** and **break the circuit** the same as **switch it off**.

2 Wrap the popsicle sticks with aluminum foil and push one into the slot of each lemon.

3 Push one piece of copper tube into each lemon.

4 Use paper clips to attach the wires.

5 Open your display device to remove the battery and reveal the terminals. This calculator has a red wire marked + and a black wire marked –.

6 Connect the + wire to aluminum and the – wire to copper. In between, make sure copper connects to aluminum.

What's going on?

If we've made all the right connections, after a few minutes we should see the display come on. Make sure all the switches are on!

Our lemon battery is producing a charge by having two different metals (aluminum and copper) in an acid liquid (the juice of the lemon). A chemical reaction takes place that also produces an electrical charge. The electricity is conducted through the lemon juice, into the metal and on into the circuit.

What else can you do?

Try different fruits and vegetables!

Jargon Buster

+ means **positive** and – means **negative**. Current in a circuit flows from the terminal marked positive to the one marked negative.

Warning: This Page Is Alarmed!

Now that we know how to make a circuit with a battery, lamp and switch, it's time to put our knowledge to good use!

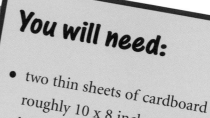

35 minutes

The plan

We are going to make a simple alarm system. It's meant to be set off by an intruder stepping on a special switch, called a pressure mat.

You will need:

- two thin sheets of cardboard roughly 10 x 8 inches (250 x 200 mm), bigger if you like
- two sheets of tin foil – the same area as the cardboard
- thin sponge sheet (sold in craft shops)
- two paper clips
- two long pieces of wire, with stripped ends
- the circuit from page 13
- glue stick, rubber cement
- small buzzer

What to do:

1 Stick foil to both sheets of cardboard.

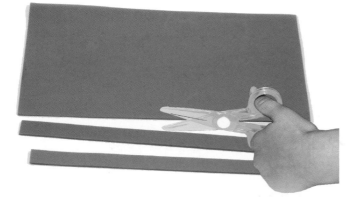

2 Cut the sponge into strips .5 inch (12 mm) wide.

3 Stick the sponge strips on one foil-covered sheet with a glue stick.

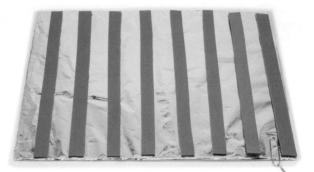

4 Put a paper clip on the edge of the foil. Attach a long wire to the paper clip.

5 Put a paper clip with a long wire on the other sheet.

6 Use tape to join the two sheets together, foil side in. Make sure the paper clips and bare wires can't touch accidentally. This is your new switch.

7 Remove the paper clip and connect the switch to the thumbtacks. Put a buzzer where the lamp was.

8 We've put the new switch under a mat.

Buuzzzzz zzzz...

What's going on?

The weight of someone stepping on the pad will complete the circuit and set off the alarm.

What else can you do?

You can make a similar switch that closes when a weight is taken off it.

Attractive Stuff

15 minutes

There's a close connection between electricity and another natural force, magnetism. Before we find out more about this connection, we need to look at magnets, what they are and how they are made.

You will need:

- at least one magnet or as many kinds of magnet as you can get
- iron filings
- some objects to test for magnetism, including some made of metal
- a hammer and a piece of scrap wood

The plan

We're going to find out more about the force of magnetism and what it can do.

Experiment 1

1 Take a magnet and find out which kind of thing is *attracted* to it.

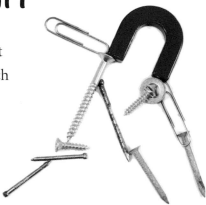

2 The objects on the right are attracted to the magnet, those on the left are not.

Jargon Buster
A **permanent** magnet means one that does not lose its magnetism after a short time.

3 It seems that all the things that the magnet will pick up are metal. But not all metal things are magnetic. Try the magnet with some aluminum foil.

4 You can use iron filings to see that the effect is strongest nearest to the magnet and that a pattern forms between one end and the other.

What's going on?

All things that are magnetic have iron in them.

Experiment 2

You can use a magnet to make a new one.

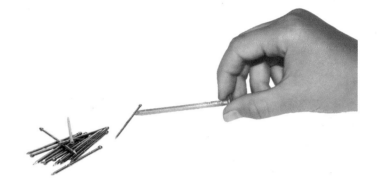

1 Take a nail and stroke it lengthwise with one end of the magnet, lifting it away at the end, always using the same end of the magnet.

2 The new magnet won't be as strong as the one that made it, but it can still pick things up!

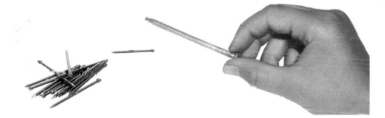

3 Put the magnetized nail on a firm surface and tap it with a hammer along its length. Try not to bend it!

4 We have destroyed the magnetism in the nail.

What's going on?

Nails are made of iron in which the *molecules* are like little magnets arranged randomly. The effect of all the little magnets is to cancel out each other's magnetism. A magnet works because its molecules are all pointing the same way. Stroking a piece of iron (the nail) with a magnet gradually lines up the molecules, magnetizing it. Hitting the nail with a hammer jars the molecules back into their random arrangement, destroying the magnetic effect.

Invisible Forces

Let's look a little more closely at what magnetism can do.

The plan

We are going to look at the ability of magnetism to pass through materials.

Experiment 1

1 Copy the maze onto your board. You and a friend will each need a magnet and paper clip.

30 minutes

You will need:

- two magnets
- a sheet of thin cardboard the same size as a piece of office paper
- marker
- two paper clips of different colors
- a plain glass jar with a plastic lid, clear sides and no labels
- paper, colored pencils or markers, scissors, tape
- a clean, flat baking tray (check that a magnet will stick to it)

2 Starting at opposite ends, you both guide your paper clip through the maze using magnets under the cardboard. Each of you chooses an entrance and aims for the exit on the other side. When you've finished, try playing the game again, but this time with the cardboard on a metal baking tray. Will the game still work?

Experiment 2

1 Do the magic snake trick and baffle your friends! Copy the snake onto paper. Make it a little smaller if necessary, so that it fits in the bottom of the glass jar. Color and cut out the snake.

2 Put a paper clip on the snake's head.

3 Stick the tip of the tail to the bottom of the jar.

4 Secretly hold a magnet in the palm of your hand as you gently turn the jar upside down and back again.

5 The snake stays up!

6 Take your hand away (with the magnet) and the snake falls down.

What's going on?

In experiment 1, magnetism passes through the cardboard easily but not through metal. In experiment 2, the snake trick reminds us that just because we can't see something (magnetism), it doesn't mean there's nothing there.

Jargon Buster

A **magnetic field** is the space around a magnet in which magnetism can be detected.

North and South

25 minutes

Magnets are often marked "N" and "S" at the ends. We call these *poles*, but what does this mean?

The plan

We're going to see how magnets behave together and find out how to tell which pole is which.

You will need:

- 2 bar magnets
- a small compass
- paper and pencil
- some thread
- magnetic toy train

Experiment 1

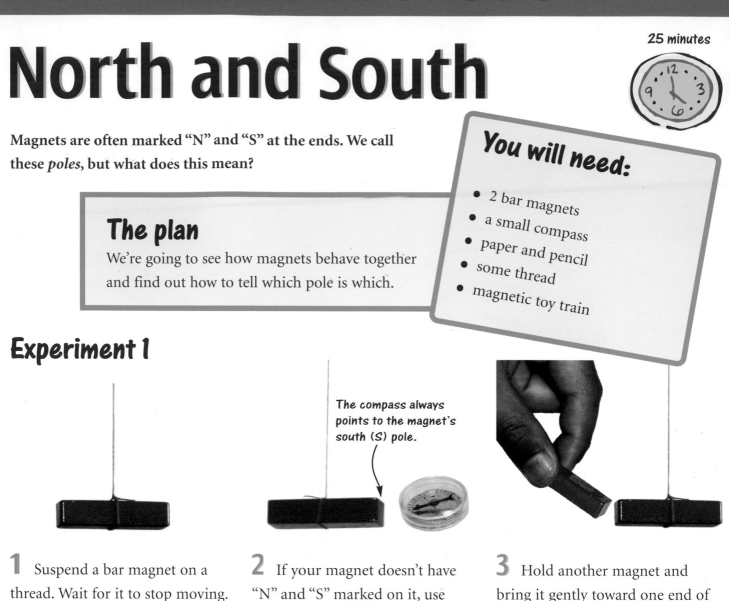

The compass always points to the magnet's south (S) pole.

1 Suspend a bar magnet on a thread. Wait for it to stop moving.

2 If your magnet doesn't have "N" and "S" marked on it, use your small compass to find out which end is which.

3 Hold another magnet and bring it gently toward one end of the first magnet.

4 The hanging magnet will either <u>attract</u> or *repel* the other magnet.

5 Try all the ways of putting the magnets' ends together. There are four. You get results like these.

$$N + N = \text{repel} \qquad S + S = \text{repel}$$
$$N + S = \text{attract} \qquad S + N = \text{attract}$$

What's going on?

Unlike poles attract and like poles repel.

Experiment 2

1 If you have a younger brother or sister, he or she might have a toy train like this one with magnetic couplings. Can we explain why the train will stay together if the cars are the right way, and why it will come apart if they are not?

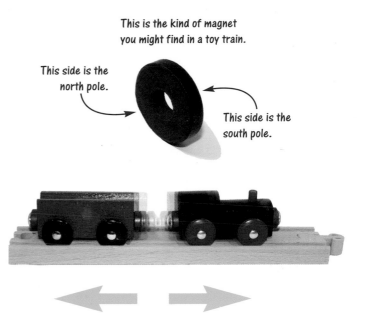

This is the kind of magnet you might find in a toy train.

This side is the north pole.

This side is the south pole.

2 If you have a magnet with poles marked on it, you can test whether the magnets on the train have north poles or south poles facing out.

Knowing that like poles repel, this end of the car must have the north pole of its magnet facing out.

Turn the magnet around, the car will now come back along the track. Unlike poles attract.

What's going on?

If we know the *polarity* of one magnet, it can tell us the polarity of others. The pointer in a compass is a little magnet. The end that points to north is actually the north pole of the pointer.

Jargon Buster
Polarity means which way around a magnet is.

The Magnetic Earth

35 minutes

A magnet has a north pole and a south pole and so does the Earth. What's the connection?

The plan

We are going to experiment with some magnets and a simple compass.

You will need:

- bar magnets
- a scrap of paper
- a small compass
- paper and pencil
- glass of water
- a needle, thread

Experiment 1

1 Magnetize a needle like the nail on page 23.

2 Thread it through some paper, like this.

What's going on?

Inside the Earth, there are large amounts of iron. It's a huge magnet and our very small needle magnet is reacting with it.

3 Float it in a glass of water.

4 The needle will turn around until it settles, pointing north.

Experiment 2

1 Put a magnet on some paper and draw around it so that you can put it back if it gets moved.

2 Move a compass around the magnet in small steps. Draw arrows in each position to show the direction of the compass needle.

3 Continue drawing arrows all around the magnet.

4 The arrows are beginning to form a pattern.

5 Join up the little arrows to make curved lines.

What's going on

You've drawn a map of a magnetic field! The magnetic field around the Earth is very similar.

Electromagnets

Here are two experiments that show the connection between electricity and magnetism.

20 minutes

The plan

We're going to use electricity to make magnets.

Experiment 1

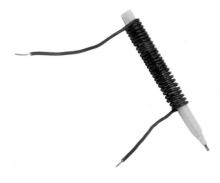

1 Wind the insulated wire tightly around the pen to make a coil.

2 Slide the pen out and connect the coil next to the lamp and switch on.

3 The lamp should come on, showing that current is flowing in the circuit. Test the coil with a magnet.

Experiment 2

1 Make sure the nail isn't magnetic. Put it into the coil in the circuit as in step 3 above. Switch on the current.

2 After 10 minutes, turn off the current, take the nail out of the coil and test with the compass.

What's going on?

In experiment 1, electricity flowing through the wire has a tiny magnetic field around it. When the wire is coiled, the effect is concentrated and produces a magnetic field. In experiment 2, the magnetic field magnetizes the nail.

Glossary

attract   (uh-TRAKT) To pull closer.

bar magnet   (BAHR MAG-net) A type of straight magnet, with north and south poles at the ends.

battery   (BA-tuh-ree) A store of electrical energy with negative and positive terminals.

buzzer   (BUH-zer) An audio signaling device, usually electronic, often used in the home, for example, in microwave ovens.

circuit   (SER-ket) An electrical circuit is a network that has a closed loop, giving a return path for the current.

compass   (KUM-pus) An instrument for finding directions on the Earth. It consists of a magnetized arrow that always points north.

conductor   (kun-DUK-ter) In science, a conductor is a material with low resistance, which means electricity can travel through it easily.

in parallel   (IN PAR-uh-lel) If two or more circuit components are connected like the rungs of a ladder, it is said that they are connected in parallel.

in series   (IN SIR-eez) If two or more circuit components are connected end to end, it is said that they are connected in series.

insulator   (INT-suh-lay-tur) A material that resists or prevents the flow of electric current, for example, rubber.

iron filings   (EYE-urn FY-lingz) Very small pieces of iron that look like a dark powder. They are sometimes used in magnetism demonstrations to show a magnetic field.

magnet   (MAG-net) A material or object that produces a magnetic field.

magnetism   (MAG-nuh-tih-zum) A way that a material attracts or repels another material.

molecules   (MAH-lih-kyoolz) The smallest units of a compound formed by atoms bonded together.

polarity   (poh-LER-uh-tee) Electricity and magnets have polarity. It's the direction that current flows in a circuit, or which way around a magnet is.

poles   (POHLZ) The ends of a magnet, north and south, where the magnetic forces are strongest.

repel   (rih-PEL) To push away.

sockets   (SO-kets) The openings into which certain things fit.

Index

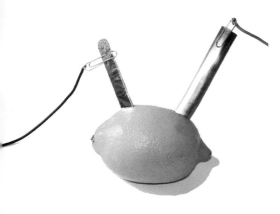

Web Sites

Due to the changing nature of Internet links, PowerKids Press has developed an online list of Web sites related to the subject of this book. This site is updated regularly. Please use this link to access the list:

www.powerkidslinks.com/scilab/elecmag/